T0130344

Nevaeh's Big Family

Jaclogne Coleman and Sean Coleman

To order additional copies of this book, contact:
Xlibris
844-714-8691
www.Xlibris.com
Orders@Xlibris.com

ISBN: Softcover 978-1-6698-1066-7
EBook 978-1-6698-1067-4

Print information available on the last page

Rev. date: 02/18/2022

Nevaeh's
Big Family

"I sure wish I had someone to play with like my oth[er] friends who have cousins and sisters and brother[s.] I wonder if I have those kind of people too," say[s] Nevaeh inquisitivel[y.]

Mommy, I am bored, I've already played with all my toys and puzzles, and you and daddy are too busy to play.... how come I don't have any sisters and brothers and cousins to play with?

"Well Nevaeh, you don't have any brothers or sisters because mommy & daddy wanted to save alllllllllllll of our hugs and kisses and tickles just for you...

4

But you do have a very big family full of aunts, uncles, and cousins on mom's side and on daddy's side too and all together they make up one big family that you can play with.

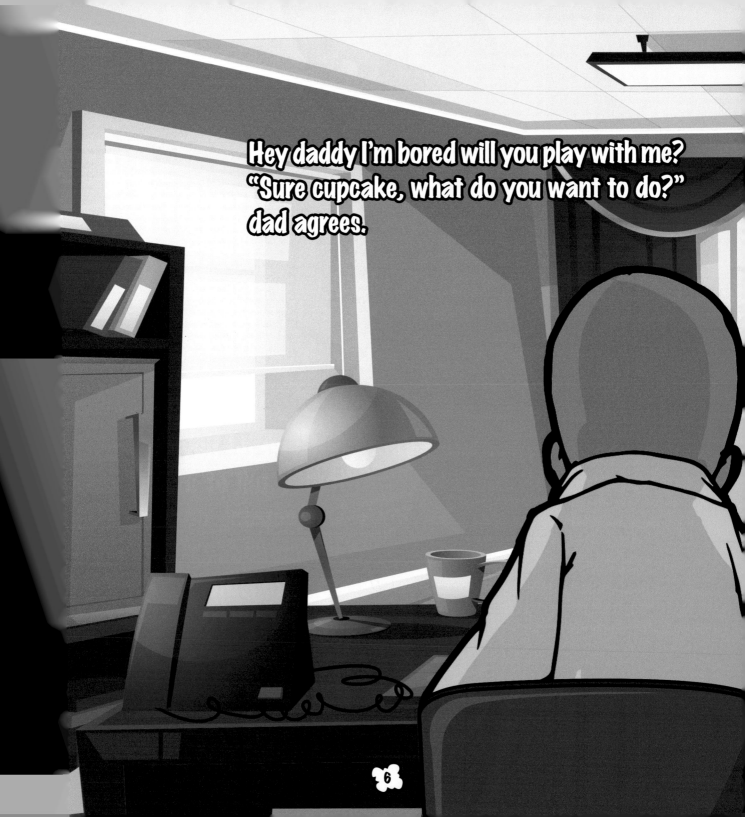

Hey daddy I'm bored will you play with me?
"Sure cupcake, what do you want to do?"
dad agrees.

9

"Also there is Uncle Toni, Uncle Don, Auntie Sandra, Auntie Sahmetra, Granny Argitha and her husband John and Aunite Tamera".

Yeah cupcake and look at these pictures you have a big family on daddy's side also, you have met them before but you were a small cupcake then.

"Well Nevaeh, they all live in other states but we can surely go visit them when you are on Spring or Summer break."

13

"Yeah you can play with your cousins Jade, Tenah, Rosie, and so many more I can't even name," says mom.

Yeah and when they visit us they can sleep in my fort and play with all my doll houses and games too and I will share my dolls and cooking set with Alvaro and all the other ones if they visit. Do you think they will visit mommy?

14

"I'm sure they will," admits Momma, "we just have to plan all these very special play dates."

wow daddy I have lots of family I wish I could play with them all

Yes you do, you have very big family that loves you very much just like we do. For summer break we will go and visit them so you can play and have fun with your cousins'. Ok goodnight....

As daddy tucks Nevaeh in she is ecstatic and imagines her big happy family.

I have a very big family, i can't wait to see and play with them all....

"Oh boy daddy I can't wait for this summer to play with all my cousins and to visit my aunts, uncles just everyone!

"Auntie tamera, granny, cousin Rosie, Uncle Henry, Uncle Nabal, Uncle Don, Auntie Sally, zzzzzzz"

Printed in the United States
by Baker & Taylor Publisher Services